REFLECTIONS OF LIFE

In this collection of verse, Gary Kempsey creates a myriad of emotions as he studies the cycle of life; from the safe innocence of childhood, through the carefree brashness of youth to the worldly wisdom that maturity brings.

For Lisette, my wife.
Dreams and reality can be very different, but for you.

REFLECTIONS OF LIFE

Gary Kempsey

ARTHUR H. STOCKWELL LTD.
Elms Court   Ilfracombe   Devon
Established 1898

*British Library Cataloguing-in-Publication Data.
A catalogue record for this book is available
from the British Library.*

ISBN 0 7223 3449-4
*Printed in Great Britain by
Arthur H. Stockwell Ltd.
Elms Court   Ilfracombe
Devon*

CONTENTS

LOOK AT ME

Look at me, what do you see,
A tall man, a thin man; is that what you see?
Look at me, what do you see,
A happy man, a sad man; which one is me?
Look at me, what do you see;
A rich man, a poor man, a man's man or a boy's man?
Look at me, what do you see;
A loving man, a sharing man or a hard and not caring man?
Look at me, what do you see;
Someone's son, someone's brother, a father or a lover?
Look at me, what do you see?
For when you look, you don't see me.

BYGONES

Remember the good times, remember the bad,
Revisit your past times, and tell me you're glad.
For when I was a young lad, it seemed such a joy
To laugh, to cry, without knowing why.
I had no comprehension of the world going by,
As it seemed to miss me in the blink of an eye.

Now I'm much older, with brood of my own,
My reflections on life, cannot be my own.
To keep them so vibrant, it must be my goal,
For wherever their life is, that is my own.

DO YOU RECALL?

When your eyes sparkle, it's a joy to see,
All of life's wonders, your love for me.
Do you remember? Do you recall,
That night we first met, the start of it all?

Two lost souls, trying to find,
Their purpose in life, their ultimate goal.
Do you remember? Do you recall,
The way you first felt, when I came to call?

Now that we're one, apart not at all,
Our life is so precious, I cherish it all.
Do you remember? Do you recall?
I see it so clearly, treasure it all.
I wonder if you do? Do you recall?

EVERYONE GOES

Everyone goes, no matter what,
Try as you do, you lose the plot.
Time will pass by you, as hard as it seems,
If you don't keep up, you'll lose your dreams.
Love is a lifetime, maybe time better spent,
To feel so much sorrow, surely wasn't meant?

Everyone leaves, for better, for worse,
I remember the lines, chapter and verse.
Morals are just, proper and true.
Have you the same values, as the one next to you?
Maybe it's destined, that such shall be,
I can't help the feeling, of anger in me.

Everyone hurts, it's true, not just me;
Circumstances are different, to you and to me.
But when it's all over, and it seemed as a dream,
Is your life so contrary, tell me please?
Class has no meaning, when life lets you down.
Who was the fool, to act like a clown?

MISSING YOU

Just an ode, to let you know, how much I miss you so.
When you're not here, I miss you dear.
I'm sure by now you know.

It must be said, when I'm in bed,
That's when I miss you most.
My life has changed, it is so strange,
Since you've been by my side.

It's not unknown, when I'm alone,
To sometimes shed a tear.
Without you near, my life's not clear;
I feel so much alone.

So do not wait, don't hesitate,
To be with me again,
For I can't wait, can't concentrate,
With all my loving pain.

A MEASURE OF CHARACTER!

A measure of character!
Is that what it's called?
When in the face of adversity
You can laugh at it all.

A measure of character!
Why should it be,
That you have to find the hard times
For people to see?

A measure of character!
No, not for me.
I want to be happy,
Feeling young and carefree.

A MOMENT OF PLEASURE

Thrashing movement,
Stop and turn.
Rest a while, there's much to learn.
Have a thought, start again;
Pulsating rhythm, silky feeling,
Twisting, thumping, racing, jumping;
Enjoyment, fulfilment, so vibrant, gleaming,
Satin feeling.
Eruption, completion, exotic peaceful, pleasing, meaning.

JUST FOR A MOMENT

Just for a moment, I thought I could see,
That door was open, just waiting for me.
But there was a twist, one I did not see,
For as I got closer, the door shut on me.

Just for a moment, a flicker of light,
Rays of hope, not just for one night.
To be so complacent, was never the aim,
Self-satisfaction, never the gain.

Just for a moment, perfect it seemed,
A life for both, a dream just to please.
I wait and I pray, for that moment again,
This time I'll grab it, not let it slip away.

HAPPY

Asked if you're happy, what do you say?
Fine thank you, it suits me this way.
Look deep within and ask once again,
See if you answer the question the same.

Take some time to breathe in the air,
View all around you, see what is there.
The soul, it is said, is the heart of the matter,
The heart to me, is the soul what matters.

To be so happy isn't that hard,
Just follow your instincts,
You'll find you'll be glad.

YOU ASK

You ask if I love you, well where do I start?
I gave you my hand, I gave you my heart.

You ask if I care, well what can I say?
I try to prove it every day.

You ask if I mean it, well what can I do?
To show my true feelings, mere words won't do.

You ask if it's forever?
How long one can't say,
But if it's forever, it'll be and a day.

PMT

PMT, what can you say?
Whatever it is, it'll be taken the wrong way.
PMT, thank you, have a nice day.
What woman would have thought
It would be this way?
But a man's perspective, a woman won't see.
So tell me why, should PMT happen to me?

WORDS

I spoke to someone today,
But not in an unusual way;
Just a few meaningless words
To pass the time away.

He said it would rain,
But not as if to complain;
So to be contraire,
I said it would be sunny, or at least, very fair.

The game was quite good.
Would you like another beer?
Yes, I said,
But I don't fancy them for next year.

We drank and we smoked,
Reminisced, told some jokes;
At the end of the evening
Said thank you and good night.

Later that evening, when I arrived home,
I sat there a while, cold and alone.
Having time to reflect, on the evening just spent,
The thought then accrued, those were words never meant.

SPOT

Oh spot, don't grow on me.
Can't you see, how silly it would be.
My friends will laugh, to see my pain,
The girls will mock to see my shame.

Oh spot, please go away,
For I don't want you on my face again.
To be so disfigured, for a boy such as me,
Does do me no justice, as anyone can see.

For, I want to be handsome, the king of the street,
With such an impairment, the requirements, I can't meet.
So do me a favour, please go away,
Come back later, when I'm old and grey.

SPECIAL THINGS

Special times, to name but just one,
Lying in the garden, soaking up the midday sun.

Special moments, a few to recall,
Glow-worms in the night, on a romantic walk home.

Special feelings, the one we had that day,
When we made love, in that very special way.

Special thoughts, to be together, not just for now,
But forever and ever.

Special reasons, for us not to part,
Because I love you with all of my heart.

DON'T CALL ME

Don't call me, I'll call you;
Musing words, I've heard before.
What do they tell me?
Well what do you think?
That it's all over, for at least one more week.

Don't call me, I've plenty to do;
Well just maybe, I have too.
We've played this game, a few times before,
To tell you the truth, it gets such a bore.

Don't call me, I'll call you;
I swear one more time, and we are through.
Is that the phone? I'd better pick up.
I'd let it ring, but you might give up.

GREEN GRASS

The grass is greener on the other side,
The man who said that, must have lied.
I've seen the grass from angles all,
To say it's greener, is for a fool.

Pastures new, that's what they say;
Yes, for a while, but then comes a day,
When you look around, only to find,
The grass seems much richer,
Once again, on the other side.

CHIN UP

It's not easy to contemplate,
The struggle of the mind,
Against all the pressures of life.
Everyone has their own dilemmas,
The individual burden to each, is what matters.

Look at others,
Their lives seem much harder;
But at the end of the day, it's yours that matters.
So please don't patronize me,
And tell me I'm doing fine,
Because in my own mind,
I'm having a real bad time.

Sometimes all I want, is to be left on my own,
To wallow in my own self-pity;
Maybe, test my inner soul;
I quite enjoy it,
If the truth were to be known;
A test of life, to see how far I can go.

Life goes on, a fact now I know;
Making the best, seems as far as I can go.
Grin and bare it, chin up old boy,
Walk tall, walk proud,
And fool them all.

MY YOUTH

What do you make of the world today,
Does it seem odd and very far away?
Time goes so fast, that you wake up one day,
Suddenly to find, that you're old and grey.

What do the children make of it all?
Where once we sat, they now have it all.
Is it so different, from when we were young,
Playing out in the midday sun?

Now it seems, they don't have the time,
To mess about, have a whale of a time.
It seems to me, they'd much rather play,
In front of a computer, happy to tap away.

Computer this. Computer that.
It appears to be, all matter of fact.
I'm glad, right now, when I look back,
To know my youth, was never like that.

MORNING BLUES

Every morning, same old thing,
Wake up kids, it's time for school.
Don't hit your sister. Do your teeth.
Have you made your lunch box?
What do you mean, there's no more drink?

Your shoes are where you left them.
Put a comb through your hair.
Don't tell me your homework's not finished,
We're running late now as it is.
Give your brother his book back,
We haven't got all week;
I wish for just one morning,
To have a bit of peace.

There's something very different,
I don't hear a sound.
The children all slept out last night,
I'm left here all alone.
So, I'll just have five more minutes,
Savour this moment alone.

Look at the time, I'm running late.
Can't find my shoes. The bus won't wait.
Comb my hair. Brush my teeth.
One more minute, the paperwork will be complete.
Look at me, all in a rush,
Without the kids, well that's just my luck.

OLD EYES

Old eyes, not gleaming bright;
No hint of sparkle, in the morning light.
More of a darkness on a moonlit night.

As young as you feel,
That maybe true,
But for your eyes, that tell on you.

Old eyes, that's what I see;
When looking at my reflection,
They can't fool me.

Your life's in your eyes,
I believe that is true;
I long for that sparkle,
That once shone through.

OLD BONES

Old bones, I can't see,
I get this feeling, they're not for me.
To see myself, way down the line
Is a comprehension, I find hard to define.

Old bones, maybe I don't want,
But then again, at what cost?
To see my offspring have sibling of their own,
Is a delight, yet to be unfold.

So I suppose I'll have to make
Old bones of a sort,
For there's much to miss,
If I give it a thought.

DID YOU EVER?

Did you ever cry, without really knowing why?
Has something touched you, deep inside,
That made you lose your self-control?

Have you ever, sat and sighed,
Felt so helpless, at what's inside?
Lost your ability of reasonable thought,
Caught up in a spiral, that may not be your fault?

Did you ever, walk that line,
Between reality, insanity,
Not knowing which is true?
For if you have, then you're human too.

AFTER LIFE

Have you ever wondered, about life after life?
Will it be golden, glittering and bright?
Will the stress just disappear
Without a trace, into thin air?

Will there still be loved ones,
To ardour, and to care?
Or will there be nothing,
No one to share?

ANGRY

You make me so angry, I want to shout;
Make me so angry, I must let it out.
You push and you pull me,
Till I don't know which way to go,
And then, don't understand, when I explode.

You make me so angry, but yet you don't see,
Until you release, the devil in me.
Why do you say, that you know me so well,
When you don't know the limits, to which you can go?

LOCKER OF LIFE

I've had so many things, happen to me,
Why should I let one more, become a tragedy?
I've laughed with joy, cried with pain;
Looking back, there was no gain.

But here I am, still plodding along,
Trying to calm, a dying song.
There maybe some differences,
Ones that you can see;
A laughter line or two is missing on me.

Proud man I am, I give no ground,
But soft in the centre, especially when let down.
Locker of life, is where you'll go,
File, misadventure,
A hazard of life.

LITTLE YELLOW ROOM

It's peaceful here, in my little yellow room,
With the world outside, shut from view.
My mind, my soul, my body relaxed,
With tranquil stability, that's hard to match.

The smell of the soap, the feel of the water;
Two candlelit boats, all senses to savour.

It's peaceful here, in my little yellow room,
It makes a change from the boredom, and the gloom.
Cleanse myself, clean my mind,
A new perspective, of a relaxing kind.

PARTNERS TOGETHER

My Cinderella, that's what you are,
My heart's desire, by long and by far.
You're my lover, my best friend,
I'm your Prince, on which to depend.

You're my daybreak, my will to live,
There's no one else, makes me feel like this.
My Queen for which, I'll serve you well,
Your King on which, my strength will tell.

So do believe, that dreams will come true,
For with me here, I'll strive for you.
A life together, partnership forever,
There'll be no bounds, for us, no never.

CANDLE OF LIFE

Candle burning, vibrant and bright,
Lights up the room, on a dark, cold night;
Emitting a halo for all to see,
With beauty to match, and transfix me.

Wax that melts and runs away,
Leaving a trace of what once there lay.
Wick that's burning, fire so bright,
Yellow and golden, dancing all night,
But black at the heart, where once there was fire,
Fuelled by the substance that is its very life.

As dusk fades to dawn, the candle wilts.
With defiant bursts of shimmering light,
That solitary flame tries to cling onto life;
One final eruption, a plume of smoke
But the decline of the candle is now complete.

EMPTY FEELING

There's something missing from this room,
Perhaps some flowers, ready to bloom?
Something lacking from where I sit,
Just can't seem to put my finger on it.

A woman's touch, children's laughter,
Fragrance of life, or love thereafter.
It's not visible, to the naked eye,
An empty feeling, you get, in passing by.

A VALUED OPINION

Don't tell me what to do,
I wouldn't presume, so why should you?
Don't live my life, like you know best,
For I might just decide to give it a rest.

To give me guidance, I don't protest,
But my point of view, I must protect.
So listen to me, like I do you,
A valued opinion, will always shine through.

THOUGHTS

I wish to be happy, I wish to be free;
I wish for a life that's good to me.
I wish for peace and harmony.

I pray for forgiveness for everyone's sins,
I pray for the day that life will touch me.

I long for the affection of someone close to me,
I long for the time when us become we.

I hope for the time when life makes me proud;
I hope for some sunshine to appear from behind that cloud.

FOREVER UNGRATEFUL

Taken for granted, we all have been;
It appears to be a natural thing.

Used and abused, we all have guilt,
For our own gain, especially in youth.

Forever ungrateful, seems par for the course;
A world full of taking, without any remorse.

CHANGE

Why am I not what I thought I would be?
Whatever happened to dreams of what should be?
Where did all the imagination for the future go?
When did all the hope lose its soul?

How did I miss the change in me,
For I don't recall the subtlety?
A void now exists so blatantly,
That I can't see how it missed me.

How do you see the change in you?
A better thing for man to see.
For don't you feel that just maybe,
You could have had more control of your destiny?

FREEDOM

Give me some freedom to be alone,
Then I'll withdraw to my own world.
Cut me some slack to do as I please,
Then I'll just sit here all at my ease.

Giving me room to think for myself,
Sends me into depression which I can't help.
A dangerous thing to use one's own mind,
Especially when not sure what might be inside.

Happier I am to be controlled,
So as not to think what the future may hold.
To explain my thoughts I cannot do,
For the reasons you'll make will not be true.

So I'll just drink to absent friends
And hope my apologies will make amends.

CHANCE

A chance to be so out of the ordinary,
As to give people a different glimpse of me.
Never to mind what people might think,
I'll carry on whilst they're all asleep.

What difference does it make
If they don't understand me?
It's not for understanding that drives me.

Satisfaction in your own mind,
Is better than anything offered by mankind.
So don't be afraid to express your own views,
Take them or leave them,
It's all up to you.

NEXT STOP

The world is turning and I want to get off,
But the harder I try, the more it won't stop.
I feel so giddy with the speed that it goes,
As it bypasses my mind and puts me in overload.

There should be a brake that we all could use,
Just to slow down when we get confused.
But yesterday's gone before we were here,
Next week appears from out of thin air.

The world is turning it seems such a shame,
For the direction it's taking, can only cause pain.
So please let me off, just at the next stop,
I'll get on a planet that lives at a trot.

SLEEP ON YOUR PILLOW

With tomorrow, dawns a brand-new day,
To take your troubles far away;
So sleep on your pillow with dreams of delight,
In anticipation, of something so bright.

But if all else fails and your day lets you down,
Just think of tomorrow, when your life turns around;
For tomorrow they say, takes your cares away,
So sleep on your pillow for the dawn of your day.

WHAT I WANT

How long do I wait for my life to begin?
How long must I pay for someone else's sin?
My life stands still in suspended animation,
Whilst others around me build new worlds
To please and astound them.

How long do I sit on a perch
So precarious, which makes me age with vulgar uncaring-ness?

My mind's being destroyed,
With ever-increasing complacency,
And expectations of people around me.

Why should I not throw in the towel?
For a pat on the back won't calm the swell.
I see what I want but it can't be so,
For that would require me to just let go.

OWN MIND

I've made up my mind, I'll just be myself;
To hell with the consequences and everyone else.
I've made up my mind to be my own person,
Follow my path wherever it goes.

If there's a wrong turning I shouldn't take,
Then it'll be my own fault, my mistake;
No blame can be put on anyone else,
For I've made the decision, no one else.

BIRDSONG

What does a bird sing when it feels afraid?
Does it sing differently from when it was brave?
How can you tell when life's not going so well,
Before it's a disaster, before you can tell?

How do the birds know when to call it a day,
Before there is trouble to come their way?
Why don't we see it so well,
As to deflect danger before it becomes hell?

How do the birds know when not to sing?
For if they could tell us,
We all would live without sin.

CROSSROADS

Crossroads of your life, where do you stand?
Forever at the junction awaiting your command.
The turning point of destiny itself,
Is in your own hands, but still you won't decide,
Unless given a hand.

You wait at the junction in uncertain control;
For a push in the wrong direction,
Will send you somewhere unknown.

But a point must come
To decide once and for all,
The direction your life takes, without influence from anyone else.

For to stay at the crossroads for the rest of your life,
Will cause you to think, what if I turned left or maybe right?
So make a decision before it's too late,
Don't miss the boat for time won't wait.